LOOK CLOSER

MEADOW

PHOTOGRAPHED BY
KIM TAYLOR and JANE BURTON

WRITTEN BY
BARBARA TAYLOR

DK

DORLING KINDERSLEY . LONDON . NEW YORK . STUTTGART

![DK]

A DORLING KINDERSLEY BOOK

Senior editor Christiane Gunzi **Senior art editor** Val Wright
Editor Deborah Murrell **Art editor** Julie Staniland
Design assistant Lucy Bennett
Production Louise Barratt
Illustrations Nick Hall
Index Jane Parker
Managing editor Sophie Mitchell
Managing art editor Miranda Kennedy

Consultants
Andy Currant, Theresa Greenaway,
Paul Hillyard, Tim Parmenter, Edward Wade

With thanks to Trevor Smith's Animal World
for supplying some of the animals in this book.

Endpapers photographed by Hans Reinhard,
Bruce Coleman Ltd.

First published in Great Britain in 1992 by
Dorling Kindersley Limited
9 Henrietta Street
Covent Garden
London WC2E 8PS

A CIP catalogue for this book is available from the British Library.
ISBN 0 86318 898 2

Colour reproduction by Colourscan, Singapore
Printed and bound in Italy by New Interlitho, Milan

CONTENTS

Look for us, and we will show you the size of every animal and plant that you read about in this book.

LIFE IN A MEADOW

DOTTED WITH COLOURFUL FLOWERS and buzzing with insects, meadows are a rich habitat for wildlife. In summer, insects feed on the flowers, while larger animals such as mice and snakes clamber and slither among the tall grasses. Many animals spend winter in the meadow in nests or burrows. Insect eggs stay buried in soil, and even seeds rest, sprouting only on warm, wet spring days. Most meadows were created many years ago, when people began to graze animals on the land and grow grasses to make hay. Today, many meadows have been ploughed up so that farmers can grow crops, with the help of chemicals. Wildlife finds it hard to survive in these fields. We need to protect flower meadows so that wild plants and animals can keep their homes.

Slow worm (young)
Anguis fragilis
7.5 cm long
LIVES IN ASIA AND EUROPE

Stripe-winged grasshopper
Stenobothrus lineatus
2 cm long
LIVES IN EUROPE

Harvest mouse (young)
Micromys minutus
3.5 cm long
LIVES IN EUROPE

Water avens
Geum rivale
flowers 1.5 cm wide
LIVES IN EUROPE, NORTH AMERICA, AND WESTERN ASIA

Field scabious
Knautia arvensis
flowers 4 cm wide
LIVES IN EUROPE AND WESTERN ASIA

Ragwort
Senecio jacobaea
flowers 2.5 cm wide
LIVES IN EUROPE, NEW ZEALAND, NORTH AFRICA, NORTH AMERICA, AND WESTERN ASIA

Grass snake (young)
Natrix natrix
25 cm long
LIVES IN ASIA AND EUROPE

Cocks-foot grass
Dactylis glomerata
seed head 6 cm long
LIVES IN NORTH AFRICA, ASIA, AND EUROPE

Bumblebee
Bombus terrestris
1.5 cm long
LIVES IN AUSTRALIA, EUROPE,
AND NORTH AFRICA

Wood cranesbill
Geranium sylvaticum
flowers 3 cm wide
LIVES IN EUROPE, NORTH
AMERICA, AND SIBERIA

Dung fly
Scatophaga stercoraria
1 cm long
LIVES IN ASIA, EUROPE,
NORTH AFRICA, AND
NORTH AMERICA

Damselfly
Calopteryx virgo
4.5 cm long
LIVES IN EUROPE

Dandelion
Taraxacum officinale
flowers 4 cm wide
LIVES NORTH OF
THE EQUATOR

Red clover
Trifolium pratense
flowers 2 cm wide
LIVES IN EUROPE, NEW ZEALAND,
NORTH AND SOUTH AMERICA,
AND WESTERN ASIA

Cinnabar moth
Tyria jacobaeae
wingspan 4.5 cm
LIVES IN EUROPE AND
WESTERN ASIA

Crab spider
Misumena vatia
1 cm long
LIVES IN EUROPE,
JAPAN AND NORTH
AMERICA

**Froghopper
nymph**
*Philaenus
spumarius*
7 mm long
LIVES IN ASIA,
EUROPE, AND
NORTH AMERICA

Eggs
of cinnabar moth
less than 1 mm wide

**Red-legged
partridge chick**
Alectoris rufa
7.5 cm high
LIVES IN FRANCE,
SPAIN, AND
THE U.K.

LEGLESS LIZARD

THIS SLITHERY SLOW-WORM is not a worm, in spite of its name, but a kind of lizard. It looks like a worm because, unlike most lizards, it has no legs. Slow-worms like to live in damp places, in long grass or leafy hedgerows, where they can hide from predators (enemies), such as snakes. Slow-worms feed on slugs, snails, worms, and insects. In the cold winter months, when food is hard to find, they hibernate (sleep) in groups under tree roots, or in hollows in the ground. The female slow-worm keeps her eggs inside her body until they are ready to hatch, then gives birth to between 12 and 20 live young.

GUESS WHAT?
Both slow-worms and grass snakes have long lives. Slow-worms can live for more than 50 years, and grass snakes usually live for about 20 years.

WORN-OUT SKIN
The slow-worm's scales are made of tough material. As this gradually wears away, a new set of scales grows beneath the outer one, and the old skin peels off the body. This is called sloughing. Most lizards slough their skin in several pieces, but slow-worms shed theirs in one piece, like snakes.

SUN WORSHIPPER
Like all reptiles, slow-worms have to soak up the warmth of the sun in order to gather enough energy to move about and hunt. They are often found basking on warm, sunny banks, but on very hot days they stay in the shade underneath flat stones, so that the sun does not dry them out.

The long, thin body shape helps the slow-worm to burrow easily into fallen leaves and soil.

The tiny scales fit closely together, so the body looks and feels smooth.

Females and young slow-worms, like this one, have a dark belly and pale brown back.

The rounded snout helps the slow-worm to push aside soil, grass, and leaves as it slithers along.

Eyelids keep the eyes clean.

Snakes have no eyelids, so they cannot shut their eyes. They seem to be staring all the time.

This pale collar gives grass snakes their other popular name. They are often called ringed snakes.

The mouth is hinged so that it can open very wide. Grass snakes swallow their prey alive.

The forked tongue flicks in and out, tasting the air, and picking up chemical information.

SWIMMING SNAKE
This snake is a good swimmer. It needs to be, because it feeds mainly on animals which live in or around water. Its streamlined body helps it to slip easily and quickly through the water.

SNAKE IN THE GRASS

THE EUROPEAN GRASS SNAKE likes to bask in the sun, but disappears into the undergrowth when disturbed. It is sensitive to vibrations in the ground, which helps it to avoid danger and catch food. Grass snakes feed mostly on frogs and newts, so they prefer to live in marshy meadows. These snakes hibernate in winter, under logs or in holes in the ground. In summer, the female lays her eggs in rotting plant material. This gives off heat, keeping the eggs and young snakes warm.

DEAD OR ALIVE
Grass snakes are not poisonous, but they can produce a very unpleasant smell to put off their enemies. They also wave their heads about and hiss loudly to make themselves look more frightening. Sometimes they even pretend to be dead, in the hope that their enemy will only attack living prey.

The snake's long, thin body helps it to move fast, both in water and on land.

FLOWER POWER

MANY KINDS OF FLOWERING plants grow in meadows, including dandelions, buttercups, and clover. These wild flowers are often called weeds, because they grow quickly and do not need to be looked after. But they are just as attractive as the flowers that people grow in their gardens. Different sorts of meadows suit different plants. Water avens grows best in marshy meadows, and wood cranesbill grows well on high or low ground. During the warm summer months, these plants produce flowers, which contain pollen and the sweet nectar that bees and butterflies like to eat. Meadow plants play an important part in providing food and shelter for many creatures, including insects, snails, and small mammals.

The red stamens which carry pollen are near the top of the flower. Insects cannot avoid getting some of the pollen on their bodies as they feed.

LION'S TEETH

The jagged leaves of the dandelion look rather like teeth, so people named the plant "dent de lion", which means "lion's tooth" in French. Dandelion flowers open in the morning and close in the afternoon. They also close when it rains. Their seeds have tiny, feathery parachutes which carry them on the wind, spreading them quickly over wide areas. Dandelions can produce seeds without being pollinated, and new plants can also spring from the roots of an old one.

This bud is still tightly closed. When it opens, the pollen will ripen in the sun.

The hairy sepals of this water avens flower help to protect the petals.

The dandelion's yellow petals are easy to spot in the meadow.

The wind spreads the pollen of this cocks-foot grass in summer.

This beetle is crawling on a dandelion flower which has lost all its petals.

Pollen from grasses like this one can cause hay fever.

GUESS WHAT?
Several kinds of meadow flowers make tasty teas, and dandelion roots can be used to make coffee. But in spite of their delicate appearance, many flowers, including ragwort, are poisonous.

LATE DEVELOPERS
Ragwort, field scabious, and several other meadow plants bloom in late summer or early autumn, when there are plenty of insects around to pollinate them. Several kinds of butterflies, including this European swallowtail, help to spread the pollen. In return, the flowers provide nectar for the butterflies to eat.

POLLEN CARRIERS
As insects feed on meadow flowers, some of the pollen sticks to them. If it reaches another flower of the same kind, seeds which will produce new plants may develop. Many flowers produce pollen that is light enough to be carried on the wind, so they do not need insects to spread it.

The name "scabious" was given to this plant because people used to believe that it could cure a skin disease called scabies.

The flower head of this ragwort is a cluster of many tiny flowers, called florets.

The nectar inside red clover flowers attracts bees. As they feed, the flower brushes pollen on to their fur.

These two soldier beetles are shaped rather like the petals of the ragwort flower that they are resting on.

A thick, strong stem supports the heavy flower head. Tiny hairs covering the stem discourage insects from eating it.

This plant is called a wood cranesbill because when the fruits are mature, they look like the bill of a bird called a crane.

MEADOW MONKEYS

TINY HARVEST MICE climb
nimbly from one plant to another
like monkeys climbing through the
trees of a forest. They spend most of the
summer scampering about in the meadow,
finding seeds and insects to eat. Harvest mice
eat as much as they they can during the
summer, and store the food energy as fat inside
their bodies. In winter, they shelter from the
cold in a nest. They only leave the nest during
the warmer daylight hours, and spend more
time on the ground, away from the wind. In
spring, the female gives birth to between three
and eight young. They have no fur at first, and
cannot see or hear until they are nine days old.
After about two weeks, they leave the nest. Many
of the young only survive for a short
time, because they are attacked
by birds, toads, and weasels.

*Large nostrils
help the mouse
to smell well.*

*Short fur grows in
a thick layer close
to the body to keep
the mouse warm.*

CURLY TOES
Each foot has five toes. The
large outer toe on each back
foot can curl right around plant
stems to give the mouse a firm
grip. This special toe is very
like a human thumb.

EMERGENCY CALL
Harvest mice make a shrill
call, almost like a shriek, if
they are in danger. Newborn
harvest mice can also produce
ultrasonic sounds, which are
too high-pitched for us to hear.
These calls quickly bring their
parents to their rescue.

*One toe on each
of the front feet
is so small that
you can hardly
see it at all.*

*These long,
sharp claws
help the harvest
mouse to grip
plant stems.*

*The long toe works
like a thumb to hold
on to things.*

Long, sensitive whiskers for feeling the way, especially in the dark

Harvest mice have sharp hearing. They use their ears to listen out for insects to eat, and for enemies to escape from.

A rounded snout hides teeth sharp enough to bite through leaves and stems.

EXTRA HAND

The harvest mouse can coil the end of its tail around almost anything. This gives it extra support when it is sitting or climbing in the grass, and acts like an extra hand. A harvest mouse can hang upside down on a stem by its tail alone. When the mouse climbs upwards, it holds its tail stiffly out to help it keep its balance. Many kinds of monkeys also have a tail like this. It is called a prehensile tail.

Every hair on the mouse's body helps it to feel things.

WEAVING A HOME

Harvest mice build nests for themselves and their young to shelter in. They bite strands of grass with their sharp teeth, and weave them into a neat, round nest about the size of a tennis ball. The mouse leaves the strands joined to the grass stems so that the nest hangs in mid-air. Inside is a cosy bed of finely chewed grass or thistle down to keep the mouse and its young warm.

The long tail is much less furry than the rest of the body. This allows it to grip things more easily.

GUESS WHAT?

Harvest mice are among the smallest mice in the world. A fully grown male weighs only 7 grams, and measures just 16 cm from its head to the tip of its tail.

FLOWERS WITH FANGS

CRAB SPIDERS LURK amongst the colourful petals of meadow flowers, waiting for passing insects to land. A female crab spider's colour often matches the flower that she lives on, so she can be very close to a victim without being spotted. When an insect lands on the flower to feed, the spider pounces on its prey. Crab spiders do not spin webs, but the females spin fluffy silk cocoons to protect their eggs. Inside each cocoon, there are 20 to 30 eggs, which develop into tiny spiders, called spiderlings. They climb out of the cocoon after they have moulted (shed their skin) for the first time. Each spiderling spins a silken thread and floats away on the wind to find a new home. Crab spiders live for about one year.

GUESS WHAT?
Some crab spiders have developed unusual kinds of camouflage, so that they look like the ants they eat or the bird droppings that insects feed on.

SIDE-STEPPING
Crab spiders get their name because they tend to scuttle sideways, like crabs, instead of moving forwards. Most crab spiders do not move very much. They spend their lives crouching on leaves, flowers, or tree trunks, waiting for their next meal to land.

The body is divided into two parts with a narrow waist, called a pedicel, in the middle.

This crab spider is well disguised against the ragwort flower that it lives on.

The front two pairs of legs are longer and thicker than the other legs, for grabbing and holding prey.

MATCHING CLOTHES
Many female crab spiders can change colour to match different flowers. They may be white, brown, yellow, or even pink. It takes up to three days for the spider to change its colour. When it stays very still on the flower, it is almost impossible for an insect to spot it.

DEADLY AMBUSH

Crab spiders find their prey mainly by sensing the vibrations (movements) of an insect. When the insect is close enough, the spider lunges out and grabs it with its strong front legs. Crab spiders often catch bees and butterflies much larger than themselves.

This bee did not spot the crab spider waiting to pounce on it.

White crab spiders often live on the white petals of ox-eye daisies.

Close-up, you can see tiny hairs on each leg which pick up vibrations in the air.

The two leg-like palps are for feeling.

These simple black eyes are tiny and they cannot see well.

This yellow crab spider has climbed on to a purple cranesbill flower, so flying insects will probably see it and avoid landing there.

These jaws have needle-like fangs for injecting poison.

PARALYZING POISON

The spider bites its prey with two fangs, which inject poison just behind the victim's head. This paralyzes the insect quickly and stops it from struggling. Crab spiders have no teeth to chew their prey, and may take several hours to suck up the body fluids. All that is left is an empty husk with two holes made by the fangs.

The huge abdomen (rear part of the body) makes female crab spiders easy to recognize.

Claws on each leg grip prey and hold on to slippery surfaces.

GET UP AND GO

THESE FLUFFY partridge chicks can run around just a few hours after hatching. They leave the nest and join their parents in the hunt for food. Both parents guard and protect the chicks, and help to keep them warm. The chicks stay with the family group, called a covey, until they are about a year old. In spring, adult male partridges defend their territory (the area in which they live) against rival males. Then the male and female partridges form pairs for mating. The female partridge lays her eggs in a hollow in the ground among tall grasses or under a hedge. She sits on the eggs for about three and a half weeks, to keep them warm until they hatch. The colour of her feathers blends in with the shadowy background, so she is almost invisible to enemies.

The ear openings are on the sides of the head.

Soft down traps air next to the skin, to keep the bird warm.

The down has dark and light stripes, which help to hide the young chick in the undergrowth.

The wings are still very small, so the chick can only flutter.

BALLS OF FLUFF
When partridge chicks hatch, they are covered in soft, fluffy feathers, called down. The down traps a layer of air next to the chick's body to stop the warmth escaping from its skin. The chicks start growing proper feathers after about two weeks, and have all their feathers at about four weeks old. But they still have down next to their skin to keep them warm. The chicks can flutter at about 10 days old, and fly properly at 16 days old.

These long, clawed toes are good for gripping things and scratching in the soil for food.

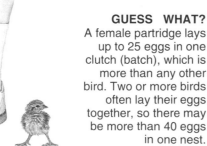

GUESS WHAT?
A female partridge lays up to 25 eggs in one clutch (batch), which is more than any other bird. Two or more birds often lay their eggs together, so there may be more than 40 eggs in one nest.

STRIPED FOR SAFETY

Striped markings break up the outline of the chick's body. This helps to disguise chicks as they wander among the tall, thin meadow grasses. The stripes make it harder for enemies, such as weasels and foxes, to see them.

The speckled pattern on the eggs helps to disguise them.

The eggshell is strong and waterproof, to stop the chick inside from drying out.

When the chicks first hatch out, the down is wet from the liquid inside the egg. But it soon dries out, and fluffs up into a soft, warm coat.

Strong, flexible ankles allow the bird to bend easily to peck at the ground.

The short beak is useful for picking up food, such as flower seeds, from the ground.

This long toe on the foot points backwards to help the chick to keep its balance.

Close-up, you can see the tough, scaly skin which protects the legs and feet.

BENDING BACKWARDS

The chick's legs look as though they bend backwards rather than forwards at the knee. But the joint we can see bending is really the bird's ankle, not its knee, which is much closer to the body. Legs like this make it easier for the bird to bend down to pick up food from the ground.

FUZZY FLY

FURRY YELLOW dung flies spend much of their adult lives searching for cow or horse dung. They are very good at detecting the smell of the dung with their antennae. Male flies like this one wait near the dung for females to arrive, then compete with each other to win a mate. The female lays her eggs inside the dung while it is still soft. When the legless larvae, called maggots, hatch out of the eggs, they feed on the dung. They develop in safety beneath the hard, protective crust which soon forms on it, then burrow into the soil and form pupae, from which winged adults emerge. These adults are flying around, ready to mate and lay eggs, as little as one month after they have hatched.

These tiny knobs, called halteres, sense the fly's direction and speed, so that it can balance in the air.

The bristles are strong, but they break off very easily.

These simple eyes can only detect differences in light and shade.

BRISTLING BACK
The dung fly has both hairs and bristles on its body. The stiff bristles on the back can feel solid objects, and help to stop the insect from damaging itself. The soft hairs covering the body are called cilia, and they can sense vibrations (movements) in the air, such as those of a nearby enemy. These hairs also trap a layer of air next to the fly's body, which helps to keep it warm.

The compound eyes see very well and help the fly to catch its prey.

Antennae for smelling and feeling things

All six legs are attached to the thorax.

VAMPIRE FLY
Dung flies eat other insects, mostly flies, which they find in the meadow. They kill their victims by piercing them in the neck, then they suck out the body fluids. A dung fly's mouthparts are very good at piercing and sucking. The muscular pump inside its head allows it to suck liquids from almost any kind of food, living or dead.

Close-up, you can see the unusual shape of the fly's mouthparts. This shape is ideal for sucking up liquids.

The dung fly holds its wings together over its back when it is not flying.

DRUMSTICK WINGS

Dung flies have two wings. These are controlled by strong muscles in the thorax (the middle part of the body). Dung flies can fly very fast, and change direction and speed easily. Behind the wings are a pair of stalks which look like tiny drumsticks. These are called halteres, and they contain sense organs which help the fly to balance when it is flying.

Soft, hair-like cilia cover most of the body. Only males are this bright golden yellow colour. Female dung flies are grey.

Strong claws and sucker-like pads on the feet help the fly to grip on to this cocks-foot grass.

Bristles on the legs help the fly to hold on to its prey.

The legs have joints so that they can bend easily.

GUESS WHAT?

A male dung fly often guards the female by sitting on her back while she lays her eggs. This prevents another male from getting near enough to mate with her.

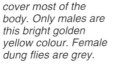

DELICATE JEWEL

THIS SLENDER, DELICATE damselfly is related to the dragonfly, but it is a much less powerful flier. Damselflies fly slowly through waterside meadows on their flimsy wings, hunting for insects, such as gnats and midges, to eat. The female lays about 300 eggs in plant stems or leaves growing in or near water. She cuts a slit in the plant for the eggs with an egg-laying tube, called an ovipositor. Three weeks later, the eggs hatch into young, called nymphs, which live under water for about a year. They take in oxygen through gills at the tip of the abdomen, and through their skin. The nymphs are fierce hunters of water insects, including other damselfly nymphs. When they are fully grown, they climb up a plant stem and out of the water. The skin splits and the adult damselfly pulls itself free and flies away.

The large, compound eyes are on each side of the head. Good eyesight is important for flying and catching food.

The head can turn easily on the slender neck, giving the insect a good all-round view.

Soft hairs on the body keep the damselfly warm.

The short antennae are sensitive to touch and smell.

Strong jaws called mandibles

Two hooks on each foot for holding on to slippery surfaces

These hairs on the legs help the damselfly to hold on to its prey.

TUBE FLOWER
The green sepals of this campion flower are joined to form a tube which protects the seeds. Above the sepals are five colourful petals, which provide a useful resting place for a damselfly.

Once the flower is fertilized, this tube will hold the seeds until they are ripe.

Close-up, you can see the network of veins which helps to support and strengthen the wings.

The tips of the damselfly's wings are rounded. A dragonfly's wings are more pointed in shape.

Bright, shiny colours on the body help the damselfly to attract a mate.

The abdomen is made up of many segments, so that it can bend.

SPOT THE DIFFERENCE

When damselflies rest, they hold their wings together over their back, unlike dragonflies, which rest with their wings opened out flat. Damselflies belong to a group of insects called *Zygoptera*, which means "similar wings", because their four wings are all the same size and shape. The two pairs of wings do not flap at the same time, so the damselfly's flight looks rather jerky.

BEST LEG FORWARD

Damselflies, like dragonflies, have all six legs right at the front of the body. Here they are in a good position for grasping and holding food close to the jaws. The legs can also cling on to objects, such as plants, but damselflies cannot walk.

The long abdomen helps to balance the weight of the thorax (middle part of the body).

GUESS WHAT?

Damselflies' wings are so delicate that the finest spider silk floating in the air can damage them. They spend a lot of time cleaning their wings to avoid such dangers.

This male damselfly has a pair of strong claspers at the end of the abdomen. These hold on to the female during mating.

BLOWING BUBBLES

SMOOTH, GREEN froghopper nymphs like this one live on plants, in blobs of white froth. They make the froth by blowing air into a sticky fluid which comes from their abdomen (the rear part of the body). The froth helps to stop the nymph from drying out, and protects it against enemies, such as birds, while it develops into an adult froghopper. Young nymphs have short antennae (feelers) and only the beginnings of wings, called wing buds. But during the spring they moult (shed their skin) several times. By summer they have grown into adults, with full-size wings and antennae. Once they have wings to fly, they do not need the froth to protect them.

SAP SUCKERS
Froghopper adults and nymphs feed on the sap inside plant leaves and stems. They make tiny holes with their long, needle-like mouthparts, and suck up the sap.

Plant stems provide plenty of juicy sap for froghoppers and greenflies to feed on.

There is a froghopper nymph inside this blob of cuckoo spit.

Aphids like these greenflies often damage the plants that they eat.

FROTHY FROGS
Froghoppers are so-named because the nymphs leap about like tiny frogs. The white blobs produced by young froghoppers are often called cuckoo spit, but they have nothing to do with cuckoos. The name comes from the fact that the frothy blobs appear at the same time as the cuckoo begins calling to attract a mate.

Large compound eyes to detect danger

Froghopper nymphs have short, bristle-like antennae.

These tiny wing buds will eventually develop into wings.

GREEDY GREENFLY
These tiny greenflies are related to froghoppers and, like them, they suck sap. Greenflies often live in large groups, and can cause a good deal of damage to the plants they live on, such as garden flowers or food crops.

GOLD DUST

BUMBLEBEES HELP to carry the yellow dust called pollen from one meadow flower to another. In spring, a queen bee makes a nest out of grass and other plants, often in an old mouse hole. She lays her eggs in little wax cups, and sits on them to keep them warm. After a few days, most of them hatch into larvae (grubs). These feed on the nectar and pollen which the queen has stored in the nest. At about two weeks old, the grubs pupate (go into a resting stage), and then develop into adult worker bees like this one. Worker bees are females which do not mate or lay eggs, but only look after the queen and her young.

GUESS WHAT?
A bumblebee nest is about the size of a large grapefruit. In summer it can be home to more than 200 bumblebees.

SWEET TOOTH
Bumblebees feed on the pollen and sugary nectar which flowers produce. The bees lick up their food with a long, pointed tongue. They only use their jaws to carry materials for building their nests.

HAIRY BASKET
Strong hairs on the bee's back legs form a sort of basket. The bee combs the pollen from its body with its front legs, and then packs it into the baskets to carry back to the nest. Bumblebees feed their young on pollen because it contains lots of protein and helps them to grow.

The wings fold over the back when the bee is not flying.

Hairs trap a layer of warm air next to the bee's body.

WARM-UP EXERCISE
A furry coat helps to keep the bee warm, but if it is cold, it shivers to warm up its wing muscles before taking off. Rows of tiny hooks link the front wings to the back wings for flying. This makes them act like one big wing, to push the air aside more easily.

This bee has collected lots of pollen in its pollen baskets.

Hooks on each foot to grip leaves and petals

These bendy antennae can feel and smell.

DON'T EAT ME

THE FRINGED BLACK and red wings of this cinnabar moth make it easy to recognize. When it flies around the meadow at night, these colours make it difficult to spot. But during the day, the wing colouring shows up well. It warns birds and other enemies that the insect tastes bad, so they leave it alone. Cinnabar moth caterpillars also taste unpleasant, and they have bright orange and black bands as their warning signal. They often feed together in such large numbers that they can strip plants such as ragwort completely bare. When the caterpillar is fully grown, it spins a silk cocoon in the soil or under fallen leaves, and turns into a pupa. It stays hidden away for the winter, and the adult moth does not emerge from the pupa until the following summer.

COLOUR SCALES

The pattern on the wings is made from tiny, overlapping scales. Each scale is attached to the skin of the wing by a short stem. Moths belong to a group of insects called *Lepidoptera*, which means "scaled wing". Underneath the scales, the cinnabar moth's wings are transparent (see-through), like those of bees, flies, and many other insects.

GUESS WHAT?

Sometimes a bird ignores the moth's warning colours and pecks at it. But the moth's body is so tough that little harm is done before the bird tastes the unpleasant fluid that the insect produces.

These long, thin antennae can feel and smell things.

Like all insects, this moth has six jointed legs attached to the middle part of its body, called the thorax.

The large compound eyes are good at detecting movement. Each one has up to 6,000 separate lenses.

The bright colours warn enemies that this moth is not a tasty meal.

The front and back wings are joined together so that they beat up and down at the same time.

Scales form a fringe around the edges of each wing.

DRINKING STRAW

Adult moths feed on liquids, such as the sweet nectar from flowers. They suck up the nectar through their long, narrow tongue, called a proboscis. When the moth is resting, the proboscis is curled up out of the way, like a watch spring.

The proboscis is curled up neatly.

These tiny hooks help the moth to grip on to leaves.

Each egg has a protective shell lined with a thin, waterproof layer of wax.

Females lay up to 30 pale-coloured eggs, usually hidden from enemies on the underside of a leaf.

Close-up, you can see the veins which carry body fluids around the wings. This helps to keep the wings stiff, and at the right temperature for flying.

FOOD FOR ALL

Female cinnabar moths lay their eggs on plants such as ragwort, groundsel, and coltsfoot. The caterpillars chew their way out of the eggs and begin eating the leaves straight away, munching steadily until they grow large enough to turn into moths. A caterpillar moults about four times, because its tough outer skin cannot stretch as it grows.

Ragwort leaves are the cinnabar moth caterpillar's favourite food.

LEGGY LEAPER

A STRIPE-WINGED grasshopper is difficult to spot when it is sitting still among the meadow grasses. If necessary, it can leap away speedily from enemies, such as birds and spiders, on its long back legs. Grasshoppers eat mostly plants, cutting and grinding up grasses with their sharp, jagged mandibles (jaws). In summer, the female lays her eggs around the roots of grasses, or just under the soil. She covers them with a frothy liquid, which hardens to protect the eggs through the cold months. Tiny worm-like larvae hatch out in spring. They instantly moult (shed their skin) to become nymphs, which look more like adults. The nymphs moult three more times as they grow into full-sized adults.

GUESS WHAT?
This grasshopper can jump about 30 cm off the ground, which is almost 40 times its own height. When alarmed, it can combine jumping and flying to travel up to three metres away.

A CLEVER ESCAPE
If the grasshopper is caught by one of its rear legs, it can break off the leg in order to escape from its enemy. There is a special muscle at the base of the leg which snaps it off the body, and the wound seals itself immediately.

This hard, saddle-shaped collar is called a pronotum. It protects the front part of the body.

Young grasshopper nymphs like this one cannot fly because their wings are not yet fully developed.

The abdomen is made up of many segments with joints between them, so that it can bend easily.

There are two claws on the end of each leg for gripping on to objects, such as this ribbed melilot flower.

The compound eyes have many separate lenses. They are good at detecting movement.

The short, flexible antennae can feel and smell things.

When the grasshopper rests, it folds its delicate back wings under the hard front wings for protection.

There are powerful muscles in the upper part of the back legs. The grasshopper straightens its legs to push itself into the air.

The grasshopper kicks out with these back legs if an enemy tries to grab it.

Spines on the legs grip on to plants.

Mottled markings on the wings help to disguise the grasshopper when it settles on plants, or on the ground.

SINGING LEGS

To attract a female for mating, the male grasshopper makes a chirping sound with his legs. He rubs a rough pad on his back legs against a hard vein on his front wings. Females often produce a similar sound when they are ready to mate. Each kind of grasshopper has a different call. They pick up sounds through eardrums at the base of the abdomen.

GLOSSARY

Abdomen *the rear part of the body*
Antennae *a pair of feelers*
Camouflage *the colours and patterns of an animal which match its background*
Cilia *short, hair-like threads*
Cocoon *a bag which an insect pupa makes from silk for protection*
Compound eyes *eyes consisting of many separate lenses*
Hibernate *to rest or sleep during the cold months of the year*
Larva *the young, grub-like stage of an animal, such as an insect*
Moult *to shed the skin or exoskeleton*
Nectar *the sweet liquid which flowers produce, and which many insects drink*

Nymph *the larva of certain kinds of insects, such as damselflies*
Prehensile tail *a tail which can grasp*
Proboscis *the long, straw-like mouthpart of a butterfly or moth*
Pupa *the resting stage between a larva and an adult insect*
Sepal *one of the outer parts of a flower that protect the bud*
Sloughing *moulting (snakes and lizards)*
Thorax *the middle part of the body, containing the heart and lungs*
Ultrasonic *a sound which is too high for a human to hear*
Vibrations *tiny movements in air, in water, or underground*